Advance Praise For Carole McManus, Jeff Tidwell and
Next For Me: A Guide To Startups For Dreamers

"Carole and Jeff have made a noble effort in this book to address the need for independence that comes with experience. They've been there, done that. They've curated real stuff that works in the real world. Any piece of the wealth that they suggest will improve one's perspectives and conditions when starting something new."
- David Allen, Author, *Getting Things Done*

"I was lucky to have a front row seat when the authors built online communities where isolated cancer patients could connect and find support from others. They now bring that human connection to this guide of big ideas for entrepreneurs of all stripes."
- Clare Martorana, CIO, U.S. Office of Personnel Management

"In this guidebook you won't find the traditional business writing or formulas. Carole and Jeff wear their hearts and minds on their sleeves within these pages. They genuinely care about the kind of business and culture they're building. They care that the people they work with share their values and principles. They care that what they put out in the world is thoughtful and kind."
- Chip Conley, Founder, Modern Elder Academy

NEXT FOR ME

"There is nothing more satisfying to me than a book that doubles as a guide and a trusted wise friend. Jeff and Carole demystify the numerous perceived hurdles in launching a startup helping you gain clarity of purpose and infuse that critical component into everything that you do as a founder. It is a beautiful gift from their incredible experiences to you. Enjoy!"

— David Newson, Principal, B|O|S + TEDxSoMa Curator

"A lot of young designers and students ask me what they should do at the beginning of their careers. I tell them to find a place where they can learn from old people. Any problem you'll encounter, they've encountered it a thousand times. Any workplace drama you'll encounter, they've encountered it a thousand times. Any fool you'll have to deal with, they've dealt with that fool a thousand times. As refreshing and necessary as it is to bring in the youth, it's just as necessary to not forget the experience that our older employees bring to the table. In *Next For Me: A Guide To Startups For Dreamers*, Jeff and Carole do a wonderful job of telling the story of experience."

— Mike Monteiro, Author, Ruined by Design

"The authors have found a recipe for startups that looks beyond the typical hype of Silicon Valley to something more heartfelt and fun along the way."

— Andres Wydler, Executive Director, StartOut

NEXT FOR ME

A Guide to Startups for Dreamers

By Carole McManus
and Jeff Tidwell

Foreword by Chip Conley

Copyright © 2020 Carole McManus, Jeff Tidwell
All rights reserved, Next For Me Media, Inc.

NEXT FOR ME

For Celeste and Revelin: You showed me, you helped me keep on, you are the reason. - Carole

For Lucky who supports every crazy thing I do. - Jeff

And to Drew Domkus the kind of co-founder you *dream* of. - Carole and Jeff

CONTENTS

Title Page
Dedication
Foreword   1
Introduction   5
Your Philosophical Center   15
Knowing What You Stand For   17
Patagonia's Core Values   19
Guiding Principles   22
Mission   25
People   28
Advisors   31
Growing the Network   34
Partnerships   36
Your Audience   38
Who Are You Beholden to?   39
Partner Power   41
Tying it all Together   43
   45
Fresh Perspectives   45

Open Mindedness	46
Mindfulness and Meditation	47
Vulnerability	50
Visualization	51
Writing	54
Drawing	57
Mapping Your Business	60
Using Constraints	66
I've Been Here Before	69
Perspective Sleight of Hand in Practice	73
	75
High-mindedness to Tactical	75
Mind/Body	76
Self Care	77
Be a Hacker	79
Sell It	82
Financial Realness	86
Lean, Frugal And In Control	87
Easy On The Dependencies	91
Do it Yourself	93
Always Be Publishing	95
Community	100
Time	102
Filtering Conversations	104
Saying No	106
First Possible	107

Email is Not Work	108
Distractions	109
Conclusion	113
Resources	114

FOREWORD

I first met Jeff Tidwell in 2001 when I was presiding over my boutique hotel company, Joie de Vivre in San Francisco. Jeff sent an email from Kauai, where he was operating a bed and breakfast. He had read my first book "The Rebel Rules" and sent kind words on how the book inspired him and his new company "Aloha Dude" and asked if I would like to be an advisor to his company. I liked his chutzpah and how he was crafting a brand for a small property, so I said yes.

Some 15 years later, I was finishing up my official tenure at Airbnb in October of 2017 as the in-house mentor to CEO and co-founder Brian Chesky. The experience being a Boomer in the Millennial start-up world inspired a next level awakening for me. During my four year tenure there as the Head of Global Hospitality and Strategy, I was as much a mentee as I was mentor.

Jeff showed up in San Francisco around that time and was preparing for a talk at The TechInclusion Conference, and wanted to run his talk by me. He arrived and told me the talk was about being gay and 60 in tech. It was his statement to the world about what he was facing in the workplace.

There was a moment of serendipitous alignment and much to his surprise I updated him on my experience at Airbnb. I told him I would be publishing my next book "Wisdom@Work: The Making of a Modern Elder." The book was a testament to how intergenerational collaboration was a powerful tool and imperative for the businesses of our time.

And most exciting of all, I showed him drone footage of a beachfront campus we were building in southern Baja (Mexico) called the "Modern Elder Academy", where midlife folks could retreat, find inspiration, and ponder what's next for them.

Jeff told me about an idea he had around a wisdom exchange under the brand Next For Me. I encouraged him to take the first step forward. We had some back and forth to get more specific about the startup strategy. There was enough to go on for me to get behind his ideas. Without hesitation, I invested and became an advisor.

He joined up with his longtime colleagues Carole McManus as head of editorial and community and Drew Domkus as head of media, as co-founders. They comprise a well-tuned, "we've been here before" operation and what I love and support is that they always seem to be having fun while doing it.

In this guidebook you won't find the traditional business writing or formulas. Carole and Jeff wear their hearts and minds on their sleeves within these pages. They genuinely care about the kind of business and culture they're building. They care that the people they work with share their values and principles. They care that what they put out in the world is thoughtful and kind.

The fun tricks and tips in the middle of the book are ways to look at your business in a new light or a sometimes necessary fresh perspective. They pulled in an exercise from the Modern Elder Academy too: by using pattern recognition you might find yourself in a very familiar situation, because you've been there before, metaphorically or otherwise.

Ordinarily I might be a little concerned that this company that I care so much about was always living in the clouds, and possibly not thinking about the long term success we're all hoping for. You'll see that's not the case when Carole and Jeff bring it all back to practical matters like frugality, mental and physical fitness, all the while working with the agility of hackers.

I only hope that this guide will help you in building a thoughtful organization with a foundation in values and transparency. I can say for certain that if you follow along, or even just try one of these exercises, you'll see your enterprise rise in a more enlightened way, and have a more open foundation for what's next for you.

- Chip Conley, Founder Modern Elder Academy

INTRODUCTION

"You have to go through it to get to it." - Sly Stone

So, you're building a company, are you? There is a lot of noise out there about startups, entrepreneurship, venture capital money, and the like. It would seem (with only slight exaggeration) that there are more books, podcasts, and thought pieces on the "startup journey" than there are new companies. Granted, some of it is practical information worth paying attention to, but where do you go when you'd like to be more introspective about what you're creating in the world?

In the following pages we offer a set of exercises that should help you see your young company in a more expansive light. Starting at **Your Philosophical Center** we dig into the values, mission, people and associations you make along the way. Then on to **Fresh Perspectives** with some fun techniques founded in open-mindedness including visualization, using constraints, mind mapping, and even deja vu. Then we come back to earth with **The Tactical**, our most useful survival techniques for hacking through the day-to-day and having the endurance to stay standing.

We've built our company around a cause we really believe in, with people we trust and respect. Our hope is that the things we've learned along the way can help guide your entrepreneurial experience, and even help you enjoy the process.

◆ ◆ ◆

Before we started our company Next For Me we were time-tested Silicon Valley professionals known for our work in online communities, user experience, and research. After years of contributing to successful Fortune 500 companies, as well as participating in our share of startups, you might say we were quite independent-minded.

We weren't necessarily looking to start something new. But the market signals pointed to something big and meaningful that we couldn't ignore.

If we had planned to start a company, we could have followed the traditional Silicon Valley approach of hammering out a "minimum viable product" to win over venture capitalists, then we would try to prove a certain growth trajectory to get the capital to keep going. But we'd been down that path before, where there is a financial agenda and outsized obligation to an investor to fit a market into that equation.

Lucky for us, this time, it didn't work that way at all.

We were becoming aware of bias against older workers in our world of tech. After working together on many successful projects for over twenty years, we had entered the aging demographic ourselves, and we were starting to run into roadblocks to new job opportunities. Not surprisingly, we were starting to see that age bias extends well beyond the tech industry.

There are 120 million Americans over the age of 50 and many are ill-prepared for a time without an income, especially since we are now living 20 to 30 years longer. So there is an urgency about staying relevant in the workforce at a time when the workplace is explicitly looking for younger talent. Add socially acceptable ageism to the mix, and you have an untenable situation that is just getting worse.

We saw a way to help, by providing a platform for people who wanted to stay engaged, and who still had a lot to contribute. We called our company Next For Me, and we were on a mission to help the aging demographic find their new path.

We started the company with this lofty statement:

Next For Me connects and inspires our generation to evolve our post-50 lives through new work, a new purpose, or a new social contribution.

Little did we know how much we would learn about ourselves in the process. Because we were bootstrapping — starting our business with no outside funding— we also began to call in a free set of tools and techniques that we used to stay open minded about the approach to the business we were building.

We started with a weekly newsletter. Our revenue path wasn't defined. We were thinking that if we hit a chord with the large audience, they would come flocking to us and the path to revenue would come later.

We ran Facebook ads with anxious headlines about the future and got plenty of people signing up. But they weren't engaging much. We knew they weren't coming to us through personal referrals, which made them less likely to stick around and engage on our Facebook page or website.

Still, we were growing subscriptions by a reasonable amount month over month. This was a positive sign for us and proved we didn't have to rely on Facebook to grow our audience. (We were never big fans of Facebook anyway.) We had growth, but not at the rate or size that we could sell ads or products against to keep us going. We were, however, learning a lot about the audience.

An obvious path to revenue didn't occur to us until Carole reminded us that we had a great story from our past about using our online community building skills in research environments. We had done it before for a big research firm along with Deb McDonald, a qualitative researcher who saw the potential in the technique. It was a game-changer for big consumer firms trying to understand their customers. With Deb's helpful advice and partnership, we decided to expand our offerings to include market research and consumer insights for marketers.

After a year of focus on product/market fit, building out the brand, and having in-person meetups, we knew a lot about the target demographic. We authored a market report based on our conversations, surveys, and research: "Understanding the 50+ Worker". The report was not only good, it gave us something to talk about with potential partners and sponsors. It showed there was value in what we were learning, and it was an effective calling card that opened new doors for us.

By being open to alternatives to the venture capital or paid user growth paths, we now had a compelling business story to tell. We started to sell research, sponsorships for our events, and workshops for organizations targeting this in-transition demographic.

Simply obvious, you would think. We would grow with money we earned from sales. This would keep us in control of how we evolved and help us be certain that we adhered to our values and a set of guiding principles we would develop.

Or as the authors of "New Power" termed it, in an ecosystem that revered the "unicorn" companies that grow and scale fast to multi-billion dollar valuations, we were "camels," a "platform or organization that delivers economic returns that are less spectacular than those of its alter-ego the "unicorn," but serves an important social function and can sustain investors and its community for the long term."

Midway into our second year, some of our advisors and readers questioned the tone of our corporate story and consumer message. It was filled with what they considered too much negative messaging rife with doomsday predictions. The feedback was our community didn't need to hear a retelling of such dark predictions week after week. What they/we needed is something to hope for.

We listened (we had become doomsday weary too) and conducted quick experiments to test the theory. We started publishing articles that were aspirational stories of facing down adversity and finding a way through it. Those articles immediately got considerably better traction and engagement than the darker pieces.

The results also underscored that "mindset" had as much as anything to do with a positive outcome. It suggested that having an open mind was a personality trait that would become increasingly important if our community was to make progress in their own personal development and evolution. We wrote about *that* too, and the positive reaction to those pieces told us we were honing in on the market fit.

So, not only did an open mind and a willingness to transition benefit the community we were building, it became the "way of being" for our company. If we were going to be a **catalyst for transformation**, we, too, had to be people open to transition.

It didn't hurt that we were nurtured in California traditions of Buddhist thinking and social experimentation. Being in California in the 70s and onward meant you were likely exposed to human potential movements, open dialogs about roles and self-identity, political activism, free and open information, often along a thread of eastern philosophy.

That's how we ended up here.

This book is a set of ideas and experiments you can use to think more broadly and philosophically about what's next for your business. The concepts can help you no matter what stage your new business is at.

We begin our book by discussing your **philosophical center**. We'll walk you through some exercises that help when articulating your core values, and establish some guiding principles as a framework that you can operate within. Once in place, this foundation will be your "north star" when working through your strategy, and is a quick go-to if you're ever doubting your intentions.

Then, we go deep on how to find and associate with people who share those values: co-founders, partners, advisors, and later, "cheerleaders" and customers.

Next, the broad topic of open-mindedness. Or, how to get your head ready for absolutely anything being possible. We developed an appreciation for techniques to find a **fresh perspective**, where we detail how stepping back, writing, drawing, or using other techniques to change your perspective opens a world of possibilities. They are simple hacks that expose paths and opportunities you may have missed otherwise.

Rest assured, it's not all pie in the sky, California-speak. We next cover our methods for the elegant handoff from high-mindedness to actionable strategies. We include a tactical toolkit for staying healthy, financial realness, doing things yourself, and the directive to start selling from day one.

If you've taken the plunge to do something new, we hope this book will help you on those days when you could use a nudge toward a bigger view. For us, the process of sharing something new with the world is a gesture that has our reputation, ethics and core beliefs attached. We hope our experiences will help inform your work and sustain you through the long days ahead. Make it fun. Make it matter.

- Carole McManus and Jeff Tidwell

YOUR PHILOSOPHICAL CENTER

If you've decided to go forward with an idea that will make the world a better place, great! That should be easy enough. ;-) Having a solid philosophical foundation as a guide will make the way forward a lot easier. Whenever you need a gut check on a business decision you can always weigh it against your vision, core values and a set of guiding principles.

In his book *Getting Things Done*, David Allen defines a system for evaluating work using an altitude analogy. At the top, the 50,000+ foot view. He explains:

> "This is the "big picture" view. Why does your company exist? Why do you exist? The primary purpose for anything provides the core definition of what its "work" really is. It is the ultimate job description. All the goals, visions, objectives, projects, and actions derive from this, and lead toward it."

It's a really simple technique that, with a little investment up front, pays off at whatever stage your business is at.

There is a great deal we could write about developing your brand, but that's for another book. What's important to understand now is that how you present yourself to the world is critical from the early days. Defining your brand is a lot more than the color of your logo. It's an extension of your mission, values and principles. As part of your foundation you will want to define what your brand aspires to stand for in the hearts and minds of consumers and its communities.

KNOWING WHAT YOU STAND FOR

Enlightened founders ask "what is our reason for being in business?" Core values are the fundamental beliefs and principles that give a framework when defining the purpose of your company. They're your North Star as you take your company forward, and help inform whether the paths you take are the right ones.

When core values are shared with your co-founders, and later your employees, you have a strong foundation that is expressed in how you conduct business. It will resonate in how you pick partners, the clientele you cater to, and even where you operate geographically.

How you interact internally also translates to your customer's understanding of the emotional benefits and experience they can expect when they interact with your brand. It can mean the difference between angry complaints on social media and a loyal lifetime customer.

At the end of this chapter is an exercise with a set of questions you can use to get a sense of your core values. If you can articulate those answers, you'll likely see a pattern that can inform the foundation of your endeavor. When you hew to your core values, your enthusiasm will shine through when you're talking about your work to others.

PATAGONIA'S CORE VALUES

Patagonia has a strong commitment to simplicity, the environment, and open-mindedness that is expressed in these statements/core values.

Our Reason for Being

At Patagonia, we appreciate that all life on earth is under threat of extinction. We aim to use the resources we have—our business, our investments, our voice and our imaginations—to do something about it.

Core Values
Our values reflect those of a business started by a band of climbers and surfers, and the minimalist style they promoted. The approach we take toward product design demonstrates a bias for simplicity and utility.

1. Build the best product.
2. Cause no unnecessary harm.
3. Use business to protect nature

4. Not bound by convention.

You may not be focused on environmental issues, so your business' core values may differ from Patagonia's. The point is, as a founder, you have the opportunity to build a business that reflects your lifelong values and makes an impact on the world around you. Never mind that it may feel insignificant, or that your customer base is small. Building something you believe in and are passionate about will help fuel you during the inevitable ups and downs, and will make you excited to get up each morning to tackle the next big thing.

Exercise 1: Identify Your Core Values

To get a sense of what your core values are, ask yourself...

What's more important to me, results or relationships?

How does my work reflect who I am? Or does it?

What impact does my work have on the world around me?

What is something that makes me feel proud about my work?

What does work-life balance look like for me?

What do I want my legacy to be?

Ask your co-founder(s) to write down their core values too and share your results with each other. Which ones are aligned? Which ones are different?

Having a few differences doesn't spell doom for your partnership-- you may have very different ideas of what you want your legacy to be, for example. It's a good idea to revisit these core values from time to time, as your company grows and matures.

GUIDING PRINCIPLES

The Guiding Principles for your company are informed by your defined core values. It helps to have these in place as a measure and test for your work. We ask ourselves, "does the task at hand meet the measure of the principles?"

Let's say you have the chance to work with a big oil company that has been dumping crude in the ocean, and one of your guiding principles is "work with earth-friendly companies," well, you see how it works.

If you and your team are firmly conscious of the principles, the standards test will just happen in the background as you move through your days. A regular review of the principles is recommended to make sure everyone is still on the same page. It's also an opportunity to see if things have changed and if you need to make any adjustments or additions. Like, for example, you have a new partner with some iffy professional associations - is that a big deal for any of you, or is it something you can overlook?

As Allen puts it:

"Your principles create the boundaries of your plan."

Guiding principles will serve as a guide for how you behave, the intent of what you're building, and what the acceptable norms are to get there.

When developing yours, think of statements such as:
1. We are transparent in our interactions.
2. We are compassionate and seek to understand those we interact with.
3. We choose to work with environmentally friendly organizations.
4. We are open to other points of view.
5. And the infamous statement from Google, "Do No Evil".

Exercise 2: What Are Your Guiding Principles?

Using the Core Values you have identified, expand upon them to apply your values in a practical sense.

Example:
Core Value: We are truthful
Guiding Principle: We strive for the truth in our interactions with our audiences and partners.

List your core values below and then a corresponding guiding principle.

Core Value:
Guiding Principle:

Core Value:
Guiding Principle:

Core Value:
Guiding Principle:

Clean up the output. Create a list of your core values. Create a list of your guiding principles. Display and publish widely within your company and even publish it online.

Make a commitment to your team that this is your way of operating and that you'll revisit them regularly.

MISSION

Now that you know what you stand for, you'll want to define how that will be expressed out into the world - your mission statement. With your core values and guiding principles set, you can begin the work that will encompass the first and long-term impression people have about your business, and it should be your very best foot forward.

For now, you can start thinking about the main mission of your company. The output should be a short, high-minded positioning statement that encompasses everything about your business and principles and who your customer is. For us it was:

> **Next For Me is a catalyst for transformation. We celebrate potential through our news, tools, events, jobs and communities.**

You will need to put some time aside to work on this and engage your advisors, especially those with some expertise with this kind of work. It will be time well spent, getting clarity on your mission and putting it into practice.

Exercise 3: Defining Your Mission Statement

Your job is to articulate what your company does and why in a concise statement. Since this may be new to you take a look at companies you admire. Do they have a mission statement on their website? If you like it, write it down, fill a page with the mission statements that really speak to you.

We found these mission statements that might inspire you:

Nike: "Bring inspiration and innovation to every athlete in the world.*
If you have a body, you are an athlete."

Patagonia: "Build the best product, cause no unnecessary harm, use business to inspire and implement solutions to the environmental crisis."

Nordstrom: "To give customers the most compelling shopping experience possible."

TED: "Spread ideas."

Now, look at your competitors' mission statements. What do they address that you'd like to address? What do you think is missing? Highlight action and aspirational words.

Your mission statement needs to get right to the heart of what you're doing, preferably in just one sentence. Write down some of your own action words, then some aspirational words, and from that draft your Mission Statement.

Action words that apply to my company:

Aspirational words that represent what I want my company to be:

First drafts of my mission statement:

You may not have your mission statement nailed just yet, but now you've got something you can work with to represent your company's reason for being.

PEOPLE

And now for people. When building your team, your first criteria should be finding people who share your values. The relationships and partnerships that you forge have just got to align with your principles. Remember, we're talking about the people you'll be spending most of your days with, side by side. Bad relationship choices tend to linger and can undo all the hard work you've done establishing your ideas and your vision.

For us, working together was a logical thing to do since we'd done it so many times before in the twenty years we've known each other. And let's face it, given the choice, wouldn't you want to spend your work day with people you actually like and respect?

History and Trust

There is a lot of comfort in working with someone over long periods of time. You develop an inherent trust, and you find yourselves in synch with how you approach your work and interactions. Like us, you may find yourself speaking in shorthand, no long explanations necessary.

And with time you simply can't avoid the inevitable births and deaths, good times and bad that come with long-term relationships. Even when it's outside of the professional realm, you learn who you can count on and what people are made of. You inevitably have more empathy for them when they're dealing with a challenging situation, and are (hopefully) more willing to work through challenges together.

Co-Founders

Starting a company with trusted colleagues has all of that humanity but with an urgent fire under it. It's as hard as things can be, so keeping your inner circle curated with those you trust is vital.

It's not always possible to find a co-founder among your friends and colleagues, especially if you're looking for someone to fill a skills gap. That's where your network comes in (more on that later), and where services like Founder Dating can match you with someone to balance out your team and get off to a strong start.

Because you have a mechanism for a trust test (your core values) you will know if you can remove the concerns about reckless sharing of ideas, intellectual property and so on. You are free to speak, think, and plan freely.

Exercise 4: Being Vulnerable with Co-Founders

If you can, try this early on before you go down the wrong co-founder road or end up in a situation where you can't find resolution.

Consider how comfortable you are being vulnerable with your co-founders. There will be money matters, rejections, and long hours. Are they resilient? When they get hit hard, can they bounce back? If they are (and we hope they are) glass half full people can they reassure you that they'll stick around when times are rough?

Have each founder answer these questions and see where there is alignment and where there are disconnects.

1. When finances are tight, are you in a position to forego a salary for a period of time?
2. If expected sources of income (sales, subscriptions, sponsorships, etc.) dry up, can you help identify other, new sources?
3. What are your responsibilities outside the business? Are there family obligations, civic duties, other ventures that will take up your time? What kind of time commitment can you give to the business each week/month?
4. Where do they see the company in 1, 2, 5 years' time?

ADVISORS

Calling in your very best colleagues and connections as advisors has many benefits to a new venture. This is your experienced brain trust that will help you navigate the inevitable ups and downs of those early days. You can't afford to pay them right now, but that doesn't mean that you shouldn't be generous in giving equity to this team that believes enough in what you're doing to attach their names and reputations to it.

For example, we're good at brand and marketing, editorial, community, and media production, some of the disciplines a modern company needs to grow into something of lasting value. Great advisors can fill in some of the blanks and step up when you really need them, whether that's acting as a sounding board, giving advice, or introducing you to an investor or potential partner.

Advisors are particularly valuable when they have worked with you in the past. You know them and they know your weaknesses and strengths, and often how to bring out the best in you. If your closest confidants aren't available to advise you, or don't have the expertise you need, don't hesitate to ask them for a referral. They may know someone who's a perfect fit for your board of advisors.

Once they've made the commitment keep your advisors in the loop, but respect their time by keeping your updates brief and make sure your "asks" are reasonable and easy for them to fulfill.

Exercise 5: Find Your Advisors

Our advisors have been instrumental in the creation and success of Next for Me. Aside from being trusted friends and colleagues, they share qualities that embody our most aspirational goals: they are taking the things they've learned in their distinguished careers and creating amazing second acts for themselves. They also Get It -- they see why what we're doing is needed and relevant, and they're helping us in innumerable ways.

As you're looking at your network and friends of friends who might be good advisors for your new company, use this exercise to identify the qualities that are important to you and what skills are missing in your core team. Then see how the people you know might help you bridge the skills gap.

Example: John, a well-connected software engineer you worked with a couple years ago.

Qualities you admire about him: He has always kept a cool head in a crisis, and is personable as well as professional.

The expertise he brings to the table: He has hired and managed big teams at a couple of Fortune 500 companies, and can advise you on your technical hiring criteria, as well as introduce you to some of his colleagues who are angel investors.

Now it's up to you to reach out and get them excited about the prospect of advising your company!

GROWING THE NETWORK

You should be talking to everybody you know about what you're doing. Switch your networking into hyperdrive. Establish your industry leadership by getting to know everybody working in your area of focus. If they pass a gut-check invite them into your confidence and you'll see how these adjacent people and companies can become valuable connections in your network.

We're not suggesting you become that annoying growth hacker on LinkedIn who "wants to have a quick call to find out more about your business". Relationships take time, and will be doomed if you're constantly asking the other person what they can do for you.

As our advisor Karen Wickre notes in her book *Taking the Work Out of Networking*

> "... avoid thinking of each encounter as a transaction. If you treat your connections as a kind of personal ATM you use for frequent withdrawals, you'll quickly be disappointed (and overdrawn)."

Career Coach John Tarnoff takes a slightly different point of view in his book *Boomer Reinvention*. He writes:

> *"Networking is not about taking. It's about giving. And your job is to figure out how you can first give to the people in your network, whether it is putting people together, connecting people to one another, whether it's supplying interesting information about your field."*

If you hesitate to work with other people in your space out of fear that they'll steal your highly proprietary ideas, don't. Making a connection and getting acquainted with your competitor can benefit both of you. You may even find that your businesses are quite different.

PARTNERSHIPS

Because you are a new company with limited resources, partnering with the right companies and individuals who are on board with what you're doing magnifies and amplifies every effort you make. You should consider your customers and audiences as partners too.

When you partner with another business you both benefit exponentially. A like-minded partner can share their resources and network, and, if you're doing it right, you will share yours too. You can combine competencies, business goals and reach, resulting in a bigger story you both can tell.

We have the benefit of being a publisher and we are more than happy to write about what our partners are doing. We are aligned, after all, and the projects and events our partners are involved with are of interest to our readers and customers.

Creative collaborations are waiting for the open-minded, and through the exposure new opportunities come into view.

Exercise 6: Engaging and Growing Your Network

Once a week, or at least once a month, revisit these questions:

What can I do to engage my advisors? One (non-intrusive!) example: Sharing/reposting something they've shared on social media along with your own comments/endorsement.

List 3 things you can do to grow your network, like identifying second- or third-degree connections on LinkedIn who you'd like to get to know, and the first-degree connections who can introduce you.

Identify 2-3 new potential partners. One tactic is to set up a Google Alert for specific terms relevant to your business, to see what similar businesses pop up in press releases and news articles.

YOUR AUDIENCE

We speak with our audiences continuously. We find ways to get them together and then we listen and participate in a dialog with them online and off. It's not just a good research tool, a warm, welcoming community is something our audience made clear they needed. So, we're making that possible through regular events and our growing online community, and we're learning so much about them in the process.

You may not need to form a vast community of your customers, but if you're making something or selling something to them, you absolutely must talk to them regularly or risk investing in something they don't want at all.

If your customers are separate from your audience, you'll need to double up on the research. Your early customers have as much to do with defining your vision and mission as your advisors and partnerships. If you ran them against your guiding principles how would they stack up? In our case, the readers are informing our insights, which we are then selling to marketers. Two very different audiences with different agendas.

WHO ARE YOU BEHOLDEN TO?

A good question to ask yourself when you are thinking about bringing financial partners into your venture is: Are they committed to our long-term goal with the same mission and values as us?

Often, if you go beyond your network of friends and family, the agenda of the investor can be very different from yours. So, this can be the most strategic decision you'll make. The dynamic can change as the ink is drying on the contract.

> *"When you run into an investor who doesn't understand what you're doing, whose logic doesn't make sense to you – or who tries to convince you to take a direction you strongly believe to be wrong – trust your instinct. You'll almost always know more about your product than your investors."*
>
> - LinkedIn Co-Founder Reid Hoffman, on Masters of Scale

Taking venture capital can make an enormous difference in the speed your company grows and your dream comes to life, we're just suggesting that you do what you can with what you have. The further along you are with a proven business model and revenue, the more leverage you have in investment or acquisition negotiations.

In the final section of the book, From High-Mindedness to Tactical, we cover some techniques to be as efficient as possible with the money you are bringing in or spending from your reserves.

PARTNER POWER

If you believe that you can grow exponentially with the right partnerships you're in for some nice surprises beyond the stated goals.

Here are some approaches we use to get the most from a partnership:

Co-promotion

- We have a publishing platform and a weekly newsletter, and we promote our partners in a section titled "Recommended". We even do it for potential partners we are courting or hope to get to know better. There's nothing like entering a conversation with a proven public interest in and promotion of their company.

- We write about our partners. If they are the right partners, what they are doing is relevant and of interest to our audience.

-They include us in the same ways on their platforms.

Content distribution

- We have content that is valuable and can be re-published in our partners' blogs and newsletters.

- To build awareness and traffic, the partner agrees to give attribution, such as "This article appeared on Next

For Me, Next For Me is a resource..." at the top and bottom of the article. Some branding can be added too.

- Their communications become a contributor to our click-through numbers and conversions.

- We are invited onto their podcasts and we include them in ours.

Partners can promote our newsletter as a value-add to their customers. They get the credibility of our content and we get new subscribers and awareness.

Give it a try. A first step with a partner can lead to a long, mutually beneficial relationship.

TYING IT ALL TOGETHER

Your company's core values and guiding principles set the stage for everything that comes after. If you've invested in defining what you stand for, you'll have published guidelines that are defined by your values. Your mission statement clearly expresses what your company does and who it serves.

Once solid with that, who you associate with, trust, look to for guidance, and partner with will fall in place. You'll know your audience and customers because you're in a continuous dialog with them.

You'll get so busy so quickly that you'll be in the act of *doing* all the time. Schedule reminders to revisit how and why you're doing what you're doing.

When it's time to grow and associate with more and more people your values will provide a strong foundation on which to build those relationships. You'll have the tools to know who to invite in. Your next step is to keep things in perspective by opening your mind.

FRESH PERSPECTIVES

Perspective is everything when you're starting your company. You're starting a new chapter here, and you need to be open to other possibilities and options. By altering your perspective just a little, you may find yourself with a solution to an "unsolvable" problem, or you may discover economies of scale in places you never thought to look. You can see something you've gone over a hundred times in a new light by writing about it, visualizing it, and talking it out with your partners.

OPEN MINDEDNESS

Mindset has a lot to do with how we approach challenges and how adept we are at creative thinking. Having an open mind is both a "way of being" and a technique that can be employed when thinking about your business. What may have worked for you in your career to this point isn't necessarily going to work in the new reality of your fledgling business. It's easy and more comfortable doing things the way you've always done them, but doubling down shouldn't be your default if your old ways of approaching a task aren't working. Open mindedness allows you to zoom in and out of focus or even clear your noggin out entirely. Now is the chance to open your mind (and your heart!) to new tactics and strategies.

MINDFULNESS AND MEDITATION

Mindfulness is more than a lifestyle buzzword or the latest workplace wellness trend, it's a way of observing and appreciating what is right in front of you, good <u>and</u> bad. And meditation allows you to take what you've observed, and put it into a broader context.

In meditation, you acknowledge thoughts, but don't hang onto them. As a result, eventually your mind opens to what is here, now. The author and founder of the San Francisco Zen Center, Shunryu Suzuki called it "Beginner's Mind," where everything is possible.

If you've tried meditation before, you may recall that the first few times you had a hard time quieting the thoughts swirling around your head. It's only with some practice that you learn that having those stray thoughts isn't a failure, it's human nature. With practice comes the ability to take notice of the thoughts, and without judgment let them go.

There will be many times in your experience when noisy thoughts will intrude. They can make it hard to tackle the day to day tasks at hand. They lead to self-doubt and catastrophic thinking about solvable problems. Being open and sharing these thoughts can actually be the best way to quiet them.

Exercise 7: Meditation

Sit on a firm pillow, on folded knees, or on a chair as upright as you can.

Get within a couple of feet of a wall with your eyes open, this helps for focus.

Breathe in through your nose, filling your abdomen. Breathe out through your mouth.

Count 10 breaths, start again, then again. That's one set. Do that three times.

Your mind will wander and you'll zoom in on a topic and you will obsess on it and lose your count. Start again. The only thing to concentrate on is breathing in and breathing out and your upright posture.

When you find yourself obsessing on a thought, acknowledge it and let it go. A good metaphor is a that you spot a cloud, acknowledge it, then let it float away.

That's it. Give it a try for 5 minutes. Now write down how you feel about everything on your plate. Notice any difference?

Over time try working your way to longer sessions. Consistency helps too. Try it for a little bit each day.

VULNERABILITY

"Vulnerability is the birthplace of innovation, creativity and change."— Brene Brown

Sharing that document or idea and asking for help or feedback from your partners may take some adjustment, if you're used to working autonomously. But you're all in this together, and while you each have your own unique role in the business, there are some problems and challenges that are best solved by sharing them.

Maybe you're not comfortable being this vulnerable, especially if this is a pet project or something you have strong opinions about. True open mindedness requires you to put that aside and take in the perspectives of your partners. Working through a challenge together can be satisfying and it'll build trust.

VISUALIZATION

"The purpose of visualization is insight, not pictures." - Ben Shneiderman, founding director of the Human-Computer Interaction Laboratory at the University of Maryland

There are a number of ways to visualize scenarios involving the future of your company. You might be more comfortable writing or drawing, or heck, even singing to bring something to life in your mind and imagination. Whatever your preferred method, you can be certain that you'll be looking at it differently after you do.

David Allen writes about The Reticular Activation System (RAS). RAS is the gatekeeper of what and how much is allowed in your brain at a time. We can only handle so much, you may have noticed. Allen has studied up on the experience where visualizing something stores the elements and holds them to be awakened later by a trigger of some kind.

"Your Reticular System tends to deliver information for you that you will not see otherwise. It could be all around you, but until you're imaging this outcome or what you want, this filter in your mind will not be configured to actually recognize the pattern when it's around you."

We do this all the time, plotting out projects on Post-Its on the wall, outlining articles in shared Google Docs, even scribbling flow charts on a piece of paper, snapping a pic, and sharing on Slack. The simple act of writing a to-do list helps make a daunting task look manageable. (We'll go deeper into this later in Mapping Your Business.)

After the exercise below are a few other approaches to visualizing what's next for your business - or what is possible.

Exercise 8: Visualize the Best Possible Outcome

Try this: Visualize and articulate what you're doing and imagine how it turns out in the future. What is the worst case scenario? What are all the twists and turns that need to happen for that worst case to come true? Write them down.

Now, what does it feel like and look like if you successfully execute what you're doing?

Who are the key players?

What help did you need on the way?

Having done that visualization, will you be able to recognize an opportunity when it comes your way, and seize it?

WRITING

Author Mike Monteiro told us "Write about what you do." His intention was to encourage writing as a way of exploring what you are doing more closely and to tell the world what you're doing. If you can't articulate it, you can't sell it-- to partners, to investors, to customers. And if you can't sell it, you're out of business!

As it turns out, writing offers fresh perspectives too. It was only after writing up the results of our first focus groups and one-on-one interviews that we realized we needed to focus our content even more on work and finance. And it was only after looking at some of the interview transcripts one after the other that we realized our perceived "main competitor" wasn't a competitor at all-- we had an opportunity to fulfill a need with something brand new.

When Jeff wrote over 50 articles "Chronicles of a 50+ Entrepreneur" for Forbes it was a very matter-of-fact telling of our day to day experience. But it was a useful exercise to publish regularly about what we were doing. The discipline of articulating the day to day as precisely as you can elevates it into a living process with nuance.

If the idea of public publishing gives you the shivers,

consider upping your note-taking game. There are also any number of calls for "morning journaling" as a positive way to start your day. Keeping a journal can serve as a tool to examine what you're doing more closely and thereby exposing things you wouldn't have noticed otherwise.

As artist and author Austin Kleon says,

> "Keeping a diary is about paying attention to my life and then paying attention to what I pay attention to.

> "I find that my diary is a good place to have bad ideas. I tell my diary everything I shouldn't tell anybody else, especially everyone on social media."

Good note taking skills will help you later when you're trying to track what happened when there are so many things happening that you can't keep up otherwise.

There is also something to be said for the analog process of writing as opposed to typing. There are dozens of studies that show the hand to brain connection is stronger and adds a visual component that is missing from a keyboard and screen.

Whatever approach you take you'll be delightfully surprised to see what emerges from your writing.

Exercise 9: Chronicling a Week in the Life of Your Business

To get in the writing habit, start with the basics. Lists are good, a narrative is even better.

What were your goals this week? Did you meet them?

Did you notice any recurring themes this week, like a series of sales rejections or multiple serendipitous introductions?

Did you see yourself using skills from past jobs, or did you need to learn something brand new to get things done?

What seeds were planted for what you're working on next week?

To take your writing public (and you should) skip ahead to "Always Be Publishing" in the next section.

DRAWING

We don't pretend to be great artists, but we do know our way around a flow chart or a wireframe. Sometimes, to get from concept to desired outcome, you need to have a concrete representation. This is especially true if you're working with a team that needs to execute on your ideas, and you and they have very different skill sets.

We have literally scribbled layouts and designs on the back of a napkin, and shared a photo of that scribble with our designer. Even if your drawing skill stops and ends with a stick figure, sometimes that is enough to get the point across. If you're trying to break through a problem, sometimes the act of reducing it to a series of squiggles can make it easier to see a way through.

Crude scribbles are fine for simple concepts, but what about more complicated ideas? In this case, other visual representations can substitute for drawing. Screenshots, including screenshots of things you **don't** like as well as those you do, can bring an idea into focus. Or you can go really old school and create a physical mood board out of photos and magazine clippings.

The point is, finding *some* way to get a visual representation of an idea or concept can help you bring it to life. And drawing (or scribbling, or cut-and-pasting images, or cutting up pictures...) outcomes for a problem can help bring the solution to light.

Exercise 10: Draw Your Biggest Roadblock

In the space below, draw a visual representation of the thing that is slowing you down the most. A beautiful output isn't the point. Seeing things you wouldn't otherwise is.

Include the things that give that challenge fuel and limit your ability to conquer it.

Draw those things that illustrate you beating the monster with the resources and smarts you have on hand.

MAPPING YOUR BUSINESS

Because we are visual people, mapping out the moving components, business entities and their relationships to each other has proven to be an insightful bird's eye view of what we're doing. So much of the time we are in the middle of it all and don't see the interconnectedness of the pieces.

There are a few approaches to this practice sometimes known as "mind-mapping." Mind-mapping involves creating a diagram of your project/business, and shows a hierarchical representation of all its parts. It is centered on a single concept, with major ideas and dependencies branching out from there. Those ideas can be represented with images, words, and symbols. Practitioners encourage you to move quickly. It's quantity over quality foregoing organization and criticism for now.

Given the affinity of tech folks to make associations this way, there have been software tools to do this around for a long time. For a low-tech approach we usually just grab some index cards or post-its and affix them to the nearest wall. They do tend to move around, plus the physical act of writing and placing them is helpful to the visualization process.

A similar approach can be used for drilling into a project. Where does it fit in the higher level map? What are the connecting points? What is an obstruction? The act of mapping it helps you clarify and prioritize.

When the Map Reveals a Strategic Gap

This is how we approached mapping out Next For Me at a critical juncture. We were proceeding with a consumer-first approach. Content, resources, and events for our readers. The money would somehow fall out from that, or so the thinking went.

You'll notice a distinct lack of financing or income generating activity in that map. ;-) It suggested and underscored that we would need to keep raising money as a way to stay afloat. The audience would not have been sufficient in size to monetize through advertising or paywalls.

As we've mentioned, we hoped not to keep asking for money and diluting our equity. Looking at the map showed us that we needed to consider other approaches for keeping the company afloat. Soon after we created the map we made the pivot to engage marketers as our customers by creating research products from what we knew about our audience.

Map How-To

Here's how we constructed our map. In the center is the entity: Next For Me. We added our mission statement in the center to keep our eye on the prize.

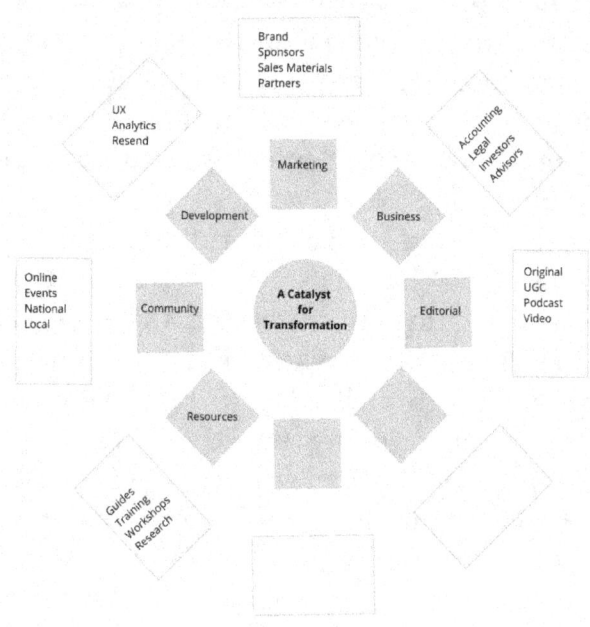

From that shakes out the high-level business units to support the vision:
1. Business
2. Editorial
3. Resources
4. Community

5. Development
6. Marketing

As an example, we'll look at the "Marketing" category to illustrate what we learned from breaking those areas of focus out and seeing the interconnectedness that the map affords.

Marketing

1. Brand: We had conducted a comprehensive brand architecture exercise. Through the mapping we identified that we then needed to engage a designer to visualize the output of that exercise. Brand, logo, colors, editorial design, etc. At this stage in our growth, there were too many touchpoints for the visual brand to put branding off any longer.

2. Partners: This has been a magic bullet for us, multiplying our efforts and exposure. We acknowledged how the relationships were positively impacting other areas of the business. So we made a decision to focus on new relationships and expand on those already in place.

3. Sponsors: We saw that we could engage sponsors to have a paid presence for our events and the research we are conducting. The outcome was that we needed to adjust our sales materials to reflect that more specifically.

4. Subscriber Growth: This is something we were experimenting with and were hoping could happen more organically. We had some evidence that we could do it through other mechanisms and through buzz with the events, so we chose to focus on growing subscribers through the events.

This exercise delivered plenty of actions to take and new areas to explore. We went in again and assigned ownership and tasks for each area. Sometimes flagging those categories that are revenue generating and riff on those.

Exercise 11: Create Your Map

Create your company as seen in the map above, Identify 4-6 main pillars of your company. Add the sub-components of those pillars

Add who is responsible for what? We assign a color or icon to each person to keep our map tidy.

Add the existing resources assigned to each component, and indicate those needed to grow each aspect of your business.

Look at the associations and see what is needed and what might be a drain on resources.

USING CONSTRAINTS

You can also fool the mind to think in a way you wouldn't have otherwise by applying constraints or new parameters around your work.

One of the most accessible tools for this was developed by the musician Brian Eno and Peter Schmidt called: Oblique Strategies. It's a series of cards that are prompts made to shift the approach to a creative endeavor. For example, "Use an old idea", or "work at a different speed", etc.

But there are many ways you can try this. Again, when trying these techniques move quick, don't judge, and strive for volume over quality. The idea is to expose gaps and opportunities, not resolve them for now.

In the same way that writing about what you're doing exposes opportunities and challenges that you wouldn't have seen otherwise, limiting or reorganizing some "mechanical aspects" of your current challenge may reveal a better way of reaching your goal or maybe the insight to do away with the project altogether.

Many of the tools used in usability testing can work here too. Observing someone using your software application or website is often employed to understand how they would go about a single task or goal. Through the limited exercise the researcher not only witnesses complete surprises about how the customer is going about the task (back to the drawing board), but they often find out other issues that didn't occur to them.

To think about it using the mapping exercise from earlier, what would your business map look like if you completely pulled a unit of the business. Let's say Legal and Accounting. That would disconnect many of the associations in your map and when looking at the adjacent dependencies, you might find that you were crazy to pull that unit as so much is dependent on it. But, you also found that the expense of one associated activity may not have been necessary at all. So, for the open-mindedness of it all, you limited the resources and discovered efficiencies. Boom!

Exercise 12: Role Switching

Switching roles with your co-founders for the sake of understanding as well as unearthing nuggets for improvement can really open your eyes. After you settle on who is switched to which role:

Express your idea of what their role is. What are their regular tasks and responsibilities?

Ask what they think it is that you do, and the percentage of time they think you spend on what they think are your key responsibilities.

You will be surprised at what bubbles up. Since you're all on the same path, this should be a fresh restart to get to a place of empathy and understanding for each other.

With practice you can zoom in and out of with these exercises, exposing some valuable discoveries which you can then apply to your thinking and strategy.

I'VE BEEN HERE BEFORE

One benefit of having been in the world of business (or whatever your field is) over time is that you begin to see patterns in what you do. You will find in your current path some version of that thing you did before.

Our advisor Chip Conley writes about getting to the "gist" of something,

> "...by synthesizing a wide variety of information quickly. Part of this is aided by the skill of pattern recognition that helps you come to hunches faster that account for the bigger picture."

The benefit is that you don't need to over-plan and over-execute because you have "been here before". You have a good idea of the right amount of energy to expend on each task. This is useful when you don't have even an hour to blow on fussiness if you're just getting a business going.

Deja Vu

In our first year we were making friends and partnering up with like-minded companies. Part of our programming mix has been in-person events and meetups. Our first event of significance was in Denver with Silvernest and Age Without Borders, two companies we were aligned with. Below is an example of how we stripped away unnecessary steps (since we had done something similar before) and just executed.

With an evolving outline of the event's program in a Google Doc, we invested just enough in advance to know what we had to do before we were all in the same room.

We had promo copy, imagery, a marketing campaign in motion and 3 interviews on video roughly edited (we cut them in half again after the first on location run-through). We wrote the final script the morning of the event.

Everybody was a professional and beyond collaborative. No egos in the way. No jockeying for a position of higher visibility.

The patterns Jeff recognized were so striking that he made a list of things he'd done in his life and career that he was doing again with Next For Me at the event.

1.   I art directed weekly newspapers in my early career - we're publishing weekly newsletters

2.   I have directed and shot all kinds of photos and videos exhibited in art scenes and, at the other end of the creative spectrum, to sell a project within a big company.

3.   I had a radio show for a couple of years and got comfortable with my voice, pacing, how to keep going no matter how much you stumble. As a result, I'm comfort-

able in front of a room of people and can even be engaging when I know what I'm talking about like I do right now.

4. Our co-founder Drew Domkus is so punk that he met his wife when he was van-touring in a band in 1994, and I notoriously managed bands in San Francisco in the 80s. We know how to work with the resources a venue has and to get set up in a hurry.

These are just some examples. We've been working in the professional world for decades. We've been putting together "scenes" even longer. We're finding again and again that we have usually done the thing we're about to do at least in some flavor before - deja vu all over again.

When you're moving fast and riffing it's great to have a foundation of scenarios and past outcomes as guidance for what's on your plate today.

Exercise 13: Deja Vu All Over Again

Name the last five job titles on your resume. How many of these could be applied to your current entrepreneurial venture?

Name your five favorite job responsibilities from your past jobs. How many of these are you responsible for in your current venture? Are there any you would like to add? What/who would need to help with that?

Name your five least favorite job responsibilities from your past jobs. How many of these are you responsible for in your current venture? Are there any you would like to delegate? What needs to change in order for that to happen?

PERSPECTIVE SLEIGHT OF HAND IN PRACTICE

By having an open mind, and a willingness to be vulnerable with ourselves and with our partners, we create the fresh perspectives we need for this brand new chapter in our careers.

Simple visualization through writing, drawing, and mapping your business can help you work through challenges and "unsolvable" problems. Using constraints and tapping into your past experiences can help you get a firm grasp on the current state of affairs and the future of your business. This is where your maturity and years in the workforce become a secret weapon, and a key to your success.

HIGH-MINDEDNESS TO TACTICAL

"Ideas are easy. Implementation is hard." - Guy Kawasaki, Evangelist and Author

Now that you know where you and your business stand in the world and have a few tricks to think more openly, it's time to get to work. Here are some tips to stay standing and give you the endurance to make your company a success.

MIND/BODY

Your mental health is so important to watch because of the ups and downs you'll be going through. We know that telling you to have a positive attitude may sound glib, but hear us out. Tuning in to your feelings and mental state will give you more options when you're down.

Here are a few things to consider to manage your mental health.

Tune in to your feelings. It's easy to get in negative mental cycles in your head. Being able to recognize those cycles, acknowledging them, and recognizing the pattern is a first step to finding your way to a more positive outlook.

SELF CARE

Meditation, exercise and other "get up from the computer" activities are fundamental to staying on stable mental ground. A walk around the block, a 15 minute quiet break and similar will give new perspective to the task at hand. Taking it further, really taking a day or weekend, or (gasp!) a week off is even better. Burning the candle at both ends isn't a sustainable or desirable way to run your business. It will still be there and you'll be coming back at it with a more open mind.

You really do need to take care of your physical self too. Let us be your entrepreneurial mother and do what we say. You need to get a good night's sleep. You need to eat healthy food. You need to get some exercise regularly. And don't drink too much.

You're going to need to stay standing both physically and metaphorically. Being healthy, fit, and strong rewards you with agility, endurance and clear-mindedness.

Limit Your Use of Social Media

YES, it's important to get your story out there via content publishing and social media. But if you find yourself constantly checking your likes and traffic, reading about your competitors, and comparing yourself to the Instagram feeds of wildly successful entrepreneurs in your field, you will go bananas. Remind yourself, as the saying goes, "No one is posting their failures". Give yourself time every day to go screen-free, relax, have a face to face conversation, read a book (<u>not</u> a business how-to!).

Build (and Maintain) Your Support System

Remember your family and your support system. Find time to be with them, they know you best. They know when you're pushing too hard and in the best cases will help you recognize it. Keep your priorities in check. You can stop checking your email when you're having some down time at the end of the day with your family or friends. And listen to them when they tell you when you're talking about work too much!

If the stress of starting a business is getting to be too much, you can find some solace in speaking to a mental health professional about what you're going through. An objective voice and point of view can make a world of difference in acknowledging where you are. There are plenty of things that you can't necessarily express to your co-founders, family or others involved in your business. Working on your head and your heart is nothing to be ashamed of.

BE A HACKER

"I'm a hacker. That's how I got here. When you have less to work with, and when people are saying no to you, even when people are saying yes a lot, that means that you're holding on to more equity. More ownership. More control."

- Arlan Hamilton, Founder Backstage Capital

We follow Arlan's lead and bring the tenants of hacking into every aspect of how we conduct our business. Coming from tech we can identify with the sensibilities of hacking. Hackers have always found ways to work around the confines of computer code to create logical solutions for more efficient systems.

Think how the hacker approach can be employed with your business. Yes, even if your venture is not in the tech realm at all.

What is the problem you are faced with? Is the expected path to a solution expensive, or does it require a lot of manpower? Is it going to take months when you don't have the luxury of time? The hacker's challenge then is to find workarounds to get there another way, another way that doesn't require a lot of resources, money, or time and doesn't compromise the whole system.

Hacking can be viewed more broadly too. If you've spent the time understanding your customers, your solution could be one that hasn't happened or worked before. To reach your customers, and deliver what they need, what specifically is it that needs hacking?

In his book, *The Lean Startup:* Eric Ries lays out his own theory for getting answers quickly: Build-Measure-Learn. Sometimes, it's as simple as an A/B test to understand which message is generating the outcome you're looking for and then doing something about it. He talks about being agile and fast in your decision making and then executing on what you learned. Rinse, repeat. That's hacking.

> *"We must learn what customers really want, not what they say they want or what we think they should want." - Eric Ries*

As a brand new company, you'll need to accomplish every task without all of the resources or know-how of a more established business. Ask yourself, "How can I hack my way into making it so?"

Exercise 14: Hack It!

What is frustrating you because of complexity or resource constraints?

List 5 things that would get you closer to resolving it without adding resources.

SELL IT

"Just concentrate on that storytelling part, on convincing people. Because if you can't do that, it doesn't matter how good the product is. It doesn't matter how good the idea was for the market, or what happens in the external factors if you don't have the people believing." - Stewart Butterfield, CEO of Slack

For your business to endure, and this sounds so obvious, you need to be out there selling your product. Can you articulate what it is? Can you speak about it as freely as you do your high-minded ideas? Selling is the most important thing you can do to support your vision, principles, independence and ultimate outcomes.

Define what you're selling. Create sales materials and language that make it easy to understand. Get a handle on the best format for delivering your sales message: a website, social media channels, printed marketing materials, traditional advertising, or some other way. Review the materials regularly. Updated versions are a great reason to publish again and update prospective customers.

Who are your customers? What problem are you solving for them? You've identified an audience for what you're producing, now think: Where do they live? How old are they? Are they going to engage with your product every day, or just occasionally? What are their related interests, and how does your product meet their needs?

Here's where creating a Persona or Personas of your customer comes in. You may not have enough data to definitively answer the above questions, and that's okay. Plenty of entrepreneurs have started off assuming one sort of person would want what they're making, only to find their assumptions were wrong.

> "A persona is a tool for maintaining an empathetic mind-set rather than designing something a certain way just because someone on the team likes it." - Erika Hall, Just Enough Research

In our case, we've obviously limited who our audience is from day one - people over the age of 50. But with time, we've honed the Next for Me Persona to age 50-65, and to reflect their interests, their life circumstances, and what they're looking to get by engaging with us.

.

Exercise 15:

Your Consumer's Persona

Starting with whatever consumer data you have - purchase records, buying histories, social media user data, survey data - create a few personas of your customers.

Then get out there and spend some one on one time with people who might fit the profile.

Even if your product is for "everyone" (and let's be honest, is it *really* for everyone?) each one will have different reasons/motivations.

Persona 1: Go ahead and give them a name and find a picture of someone that looks how they might look. You'll be using the personas as a reference to make them come alive.

What is their age?

What is their gender? Or, if relevant to your business, are they non-conforming/fluid?

Where do they live?

What is their need, desire, or pain that would make them need your product?

What are the market conditions that make the above so?

How often do they buy your product/service?

How often do they use your product/service?

What similar/related products do they also buy regularly?

Will they recommend your product to a friend? If not, what might motivate them to do so?

FINANCIAL REALNESS

No matter what your venture, no matter how bare-bones your operations are, at some point you're likely going to need capital. Where that funding comes from, and how you manage it, can have a huge impact on the future of your company.

LEAN, FRUGAL AND IN CONTROL

" Act like you've got half, because you've got to factor in all the failures and all the optimizations that really kill great entrepreneurs and businesses all the time. We know so many people who had good ideas, were on the right track. They just ran out of runway." - Mariam Naficy, Founder & CEO of Minted

We have been steadfast in waiting as long as we can to go looking for money from a traditional venture capitalist. It's important for us to be a lot further along before we consider asking for their help.

We've experienced losing control over what happens to us and our beloved companies in the past. Sometimes that possibility is the tradeoff that you take if the project is interesting enough and you are eager to be involved with the people. This time we chose to own the majority of our business and intellectual property. For now, anyway.

It means we're operating on a very lean budget. We

started by taking a small amount of friends and family money and we supplemented our incomes with other work or savings.

It's a tradeoff. If you do as much as you can without spending somebody else's money your decisions will be more carefully considered. Frugality also presents creative constraints and necessary workarounds that expose new opportunities that you wouldn't have thought of otherwise.

Austin Kleon goes further and encourages you to keep your day job, with a goal of being debt-free. He is fond of this quote from former New York Times photographer Bill Cunningham.

"If you don't take money, they can't tell you what to do."

This may all sound insane if you've been watching episodes of "Silicon Valley" or are dipping into "the startup scene." So many times we've been in situations where the emphasis is on raising money as the primary activity before getting market validation for the product or service.

If you've got money in the bank and a decent runway you should proceed as if you don't. Consider how you can do things without every expense. Is this a tradeoff you're willing to make for something else in your budget? How can you address a certain need with greater financial efficiency? Focus on spending your precious time and limited dollars getting to product/market fit.

This is not to say that you shouldn't be checking in with potential investors if you choose the bootstrap approach. Remember when we told you it was important to keep growing your network? Now's the time to foster those relationships. Let them know where you're headed now, keep in touch with email updates. When you find yourself in their office when it's time to raise more funds there will be some history. If you do as much as you can without spending somebody else's money your decisions will be more carefully considered.

Exercise 16: Financial Readiness

Are you operating from a budget which aligns to your business's strategy or just winging it? Grab yourself a "pro forma" spreadsheet template and start plugging in some numbers. There will be speculation and presumptions to get there, but don't let that stop you.

Identify the following:
1. Where is the income coming from? List the different ways you'll make money. Break it out by months and quarters. Perhaps you'll think it grows over time.
2. What is the cost of sales? What must be spent to reflect the income projections. Note that this isn't labor or costs of operations.
3. What are your labor costs? This will likely be your most pricey expense.
4. What are your expenses. Rent, travel, taxes, insurance, and such. Do not forget legal and accounting costs which can add up quickly.

With this rough estimation, take a stab at cutting costs in a way that will allow you to continue with the income growth. It's surprising where you can cut corners. If you make those cuts and it will impact the revenue, have a conversation with your partners about whether that's ok for the long-term impact on your company.

Become very familiar with these numbers. Can you explain to an investor concisely what the projections are and how you got there?

Revisit these numbers regularly. If you have the budget for an accountant establish regular financial reviews.

EASY ON THE DEPENDENCIES

Just like with other people's money, you should take a careful look at the dependencies you have or plan to enter into. What platforms, software, systems, and assumptions are your company dependent on?

For example, we have an evolving belief that keeping Facebook as a publishing dependency is not a good idea. They change their terms with publishers regularly. After betting the farm on the platform entire enterprises have tumbled as a result. Would you want to be dependent on such a moving target?

Exercise 17: What are You Dependent On?

You don't want to be dependent on the wrong money, wrong partner or resource. You want to be as independent as you can be. On the other hand, don't reinvent the wheel if there's an existing product or platform that can help you along the way.

Identify one thing you're dependent on.

How much of an impact does that dependency have on your success?

What risks do you have if something changes (e.g., the price goes up)?

What contingencies or backups can you put in place if that thing you're dependent on disappeared tomorrow?

DO IT YOURSELF

Continuous learning is part of the mix too. Roll up your sleeves. There will be many times when there is nobody around to crop that image in Photoshop, balance Quickbooks, or renew your SSL certificate. This is when DIY takes on a whole new meaning in your life.

You might find yourself having hilarious conversations with yourself about how you couldn't move this or that forward because you don't know how to do one piece of it. Get over that. Figure it out by trial and error, Google it, or call a friend, or there you shall hang awaiting a nonexistent resource. Quora, Stack Exchange, and Twitter are full of people eager to answer your question!

Because you will be in high communication mode, you'll also be asking your advisors and new partners for their help. Because their time and commitments are extremely valuable, we recommend that these requests be very targeted for a business problem that only they could move forward. And by all means, make it easy for them to help you. Do the advance work, state clearly what's got you stuck, and what, *very specifically*, you need them to do.

One of our mentors, Chris Davidson, from the Startout Growth Lab, ingrained in us your obligation when looking to engage your "cheerleaders." If you are asking for some help, connections, or for their time, Chris says you really need to have your act together.

If it's an email introduction to a potential investor, advisor, or partner, have ready: a subject line; body of the email; urls, attached documents.

If it's a product launch announcement, provide: a subject line, body of the email, urls, and distribution list. Create something that they can forward directly without having to edit out the personal pleasantries.

If it's amplifying something you've shared on social media, give them accurate urls and talking points that they can then modify to reflect their authentic voice.

Make it easy for them to help you. You don't want to risk losing the goodwill of the people who are in a position to help you succeed.

ALWAYS BE PUBLISHING

"Writing is the new resume. Whether you're building a business, leading a project, or applying for a new job, writing is how you get attention." - David Perell, Write of Passage

The truth is, today everybody is a publisher or should be. Choose your flavor(s): social media, a blog, video, a podcast... but having a presence on the internet is a requirement for most businesses. And then share, and share often. If content creation is not your forte, partner up with someone with that skill set.

Obviously publishing online, especially over time, increases your online exposure. Cross-linking from other platforms, i.e. your own blog, Medium, LinkedIn, your favorite social media channel, only increases the search engine optimization (how Google finds you), and therefore the likelihood that more people will see it. Publishing your writing is an excellent opportunity to position yourself and your work. The connections you are making will have a very good idea of who you are and what you are about before you ever meet. As Karen Wickre says,

> "Your owned content is a repository of what you're doing and what you're about."

In the era of podcasting, there is a good opportunity to host or be a guest on podcasts that are related to your work. As a guest you get the benefit of the podcasters' network, another node in your searchable entity, and ta-da, more content to edit and repurpose. As a podcaster you have a reason to contact related businesses and bring them into your brain trust.

Take The Output And Publish The Heck Out Of It

> "Take an object / Do something to it / Do something else to it. [Repeat.]" -Jasper Johns

A content machine is a way to describe what we do with the trove of video, audio and words that come out of our newsletters, articles and events. We have the crew and gear in place to "always be publishing". Take what you've written and publish it to your channels in short bites, longform, as a series, an Instagram post, Tweet, a LinkedIn article... you get the idea.

Back to the brand guidelines, we've developed a visual style for our videos and have reusable graphical elements, transitions, intros and outros, titles, and theme music that incorporate our logo and other brand elements.

And calling back to our lean, frugal operating style,

we've gotten very resourceful with a mix of our original photos and videos and free or low-cost stock imagery that fits our editorial style as we produce the stockpile of stories we are accumulating. Using a consistent style and repeating key messaging not only helps reinforce the brand, it also helps us produce new content quickly and efficiently.

Publish Then Perfect

We started our careers when publishing was a more analog process. Back then you sent the pasted-up boards to the printer and there was no looking back. That experience drove a habit of deadline buildup (and stomach knots), and then the anxiety release when it was published. Then it would start all over again.

Now we have the luxury of a more flexible medium. Carole can bang out a story seemingly effortlessly, publish it and everything is in place. Jeff takes a good-enough draft publishes it, then has a look to see how it reads, and goes in for more edits. We can always go back and add more images, include editorial updates, and cross-link to related articles.

The same goes for talking to people about what you're doing. Taking every chance to tell someone about your cause and why you're doing it provides more than just an opportunity to share what you're doing. Because we are keeping an open mind that story will evolve all the time. Testing the responses, adjusting and telling it again. It will never be perfect, so don't let that stop you.

Exercise 18: Your Publishing Universe

Are you, or is someone on your team a proficient writer? If not, budgeting for a freelance writer to help you tell the story of your company should be a priority. Your publishing universe is the many places online to publish your stories. As in all published writing it comes down to the basics: Who, What, When, and How.

Who

Think about who you need to communicate with to get out the word about what your company is doing: customers, potential customers, partners, even competitors. You'll probably communicate with each of these audiences very differently.

What

What is the information you need to put out in the world? Is it sales information, product updates, news, opinion?

When

How often can you commit to these communications? It's not necessary to push out content daily or even weekly, but consistency is key. You want to provide important information in a timely way but you also don't want to look like a spammer. An editorial calendar will help you balance current events with evergreen information.

How

Now think about the best vehicle for communicating with them. Seeing what gets engagement and surveys or informal polls can help you understand how you'll best be able to get their attention-- is it newsletters, a website, an app, a podcast, social media, a combination of all of these?

COMMUNITY

"Through open and ongoing dialogue, a loose group of people with a shared interest can be transformed into a community, teeming with life." - Get Together

We've talked about publishing content via social channels, our website, and our newsletter. But we don't just push content. A key piece of our business is having a dialogue with our audience. We interact with them face to face in meetups, events, and one-on-one interviews. Online, we get feedback from them on our social channels, through surveys, and now, through our private community.

Depending on your business goals, Facebook, Twitter, Instagram, or LinkedIn may be perfectly fine for interacting with your customers and finding new ones. But for us, these platforms don't allow us to go deep with our audience. The topics that are important to our community - finding work, finances, staring down retirement when you may not be prepared - these are subjects that were too sensitive to engage with on Facebook. We found a great low-cost community platform, Mighty Networks, that allows us to have a conversation in ways that otherwise would have meant months of development. There is easy on-boarding, a pleasing and intuitive interface, membership and course development tools, a mobile app, and much more.

We have built plenty of community platforms over the years. You would be wise to focus on what engages your audience rather than reinventing the wheel.

TIME

"The time which we have at our disposal every day is elastic; the passions that we feel expand it, those that we inspire contract it; and habit fills up what remains." - Marcel Proust

You really need to pick up the pace. We've seen millions of dollars evaporate in months with overthinking and a general laissez faire approach. You'll need to make quick decisions about what you spend your time on without the leisurely cushion that corporate jobs or too much funding often afford.

Most likely it hasn't occurred to you how long it will actually take you to succeed or at least get off the ground. We always say, if we knew how long and how challenging this has been we probably wouldn't have done it. For the sake of discussion, let's say it takes 2 to 3 years to become profitable to the point that you are able to pay your team and reinvest back into your company.

That's a long time and you may stumble, or pivot, and have life get in the way, so you better get with it. Hopefully with the tools in this book you have a foundation to know when and why you're taking time for something. Here are some of our favorite time hacks.

FILTERING CONVERSATIONS

As we noted, we really encourage you to talk with everybody in your industry. Each conversation requires a bit of scheduling and an interruption in the middle of the work day. We all know how disruptive this can be, so it's important to make sure that those conversations are in alignment with your strategy. Those distractions add up.

Obviously if you are hoping to close some business with someone you will make it extremely easy for them to connect with you.

We've also ended up with surprisingly on-point collaborators from simple introductions or serendipitous emails we sent when stumbling across a like-minded person or business. Just be thoughtful with how much time you spend with the unknown.

If a trusted colleague has asked you if you would be open to an introduction to someone, and you agree to it, then the email introduction and your response will be the opportunity to find out quickly if they're a match. Being a respected voice and collaborator in your field means you're open to the give and take of new connections.

With your new visibility from publishing and partnerships, you will likely become the target for interested parties that aren't a fit. These are often people who have an interest in what you're doing and perhaps would like to "brainstorm" some ideas with you.

There are a few filters we use to discern the potentially beneficial connections. Your instincts should guide you, but try to get to a yes/no on a call or appointment as quickly as possible.

Set the expectations of how you work by requesting a brief summary of their project or business idea. If they hedge here, it's your out. A rambling call with no agenda or even the simplest effort is probably not worth your time.

Or, if they are selling something you don't need. That's an easy out, especially on LinkedIn. #Block

SAYING NO

You may be thinking that you're a humble new business owner that should be open to every conversation anybody wants to have with you. If these conversations don't directly align with your business plan, you should probably excuse yourself with grace and candor.

There is no shame in being honest about the fact that you are focused on x and x is the best way to engage with you at this time. If folks don't appreciate your courteous response then they'll likely be more unpleasantly urgent later.

For example, at Next For Me, interested parties can subscribe to our newsletters, attend our events, join our community. We try to do business within the confines of our branded environments. This is who we are. This is where we conduct business. It's redundant to have the conversations in both places and it's off-brand.

FIRST POSSIBLE

Let's say you have agreed to a call with someone. The back and forth of scheduling can quickly become maddening. Be proactive as heck here. Suggest multiple times, your preferred conference tool, and an offer to send the invite when they confirm a time.

If you're accepting from a range of times, make it the first possible you have available. Otherwise it can lead to more back and forth and perhaps losing "the moment". It supports the urgency of your work.

Some find comfort in calendar "availability apps" such as Calend.ly that let someone choose a time you've set as free. While this might save some of the back and forth of scheduling, not having a contextual say in what is next to what on your calendar doesn't seem worth the tradeoff.

EMAIL IS NOT WORK

The quickest you can get to answering and concluding an email thread is important. Bring the thread to a conclusion if you can or make it easy for the recipient to do it. And for your own mental health shut your email client down for chunks of productive time. Answering email isn't often actually working.

We've found that for internal and some external partners Slack solves much of the email overhead. If you are comfortable with the back and forth being asynchronous, it's a fine tool for getting thoughts out to the right people, by category, and sometimes a quick response without the psychic burden of email.

DISTRACTIONS

Every Twitter thread, mobile notification, ironic newsletter, and Slack channel pulls you from your work. It's often easy to justify time noodling around online as activity related to your work. Be honest with yourself, is that really moving you forward in a meaningful way? If not, go on a digital diet, limit your intrusions, or schedule them and then get back to work.

Think about it, if you're really committed to leaving time for you, your friends and your family, even some minor modifications to limiting the feed will open up surprisingly more and more time.

As it relates to your ego and sense of place in the world, being interviewed on an obscure podcast or getting a few LIKES on Instagram is a set up for disappointment when it isn't happening all the time. Get out there, be known, be known in a way that results in moving your business forward. Stop the dopamine fix of reading about yourself or hanging on waiting for the next LIKE.

Exercise 19: Time as Your Friend

What's it gonna take to keep you on task? Try this. Quickly fill out this form for your day. Prioritize by 1-3. Estimate the time it will take to complete the task. Through the course of a day, keep your eye on the high priority tasks and document the actual time spent.

Task	Priority	Estimate	Actual

You were likely pulled into other tasks and distracted by this and that. Document those as well. What is the priority? How much time did you spend on them?

Task	Priority	Estimate	Actual

CONCLUSION

"Making the most of a long and multi-stage life means taking transitions in your stride. Being flexible, acquiring new knowledge, exploring new ways of thinking, seeing the world from a different perspective, coming to terms with changes in power, letting go of old associates and building new networks."
- Lynda Gratton and Andrew Scott, The 100-Year Life

You don't have to rethink the way you do things all at once (or listen to our advice at all for that matter). Throw one or more of these techniques into your mix. They've worked for us, and you may find them helpful, too. And, if you use the benchmark of some guiding principles, you'll know what you are doing aligns with your vision.

RESOURCES

Further Reading

Discuss this book at community.nextforme.com

All book references at nextforme.com/book

Getting Things Done by David Allen, Penguin Books, 2001

The Rebel Rules, Daring to Be Yourself in Business by Chip Conley, Touchstone, 2001

Wisdom@Work, The Making of a Modern Elder by Chip Conley, Random House, 2018

Workarounds: 50+ Insider Tactics for Age 50+ Entrepreneurs by Doug Freeman, Ideascape, Inc., 2018

Give and Take, Why Helping Others Drives Our Success by Adam Grant, Weidenfeld & Nicolson, 2013

Just Enough Research by Erika Hall, A Book Apart, 2013

New Power by Jeremy Heimans and Henry Timms, Anchor, 2018

Keep Going by Austin Kleon, Workman Publishing, 2019

The Mindful Path through Worry and Rumination: Letting Go of Anxious and Depressive Thoughts by Sameet Kumar, New Harbinger Publications, 2010

Ruined by Design by Mike Monteiro, Mule Books, 2019

You're My Favorite Client by Mike Monteiro, A Book Apart, 2014

Get Together by Bailey Richardson, Kevin Huynh, Kai Elmer Sotto, Stripe Press, 2019

The Lean Startup by Eric Ries, Currency, 2011

Zen Mind, Beginner's Mind by Shunryo Suzuki, Shambhala Library, 2006

Boomer Reinvention by John Tarnoff, Reinvention Press, 2017

Taking the Work Out of Networking, An Introvert's Guide to Making Connections That Count by Karen Wickre, Gallery Books, 2018

Recommended Podcasts

Listening to other entrepreneurs talk about their successes-- and failures! -- can be just the ticket when you're feeling alone in your startup bubble. Some stories may even help you figure out how to tackle a problem in a way you may not have thought of before.

How I Built This

Without Fail

Masters of Scale

We mentioned how guesting on podcasts can be a great way to connect with others in your field and position yourself as a thought leader. These articles will help you pitch yourself to podcast producers:

How to Pitch Podcasts

The Art of the Pitch

How to Pitch Yourself to Be a Podcast Guest

Other resources

As a lean startup, we are big fans of free and low-cost tools.

No graphic design skills? **Canva** is a wonderful platform for creating flyers, brochures, and social media posts -- even animation!

We've worked with Wordpress for years, and we're lucky to have a co-founder who is a wiz at managing the many plug-ins we use. They have hosted as well as enterprise solutions.

If the thought of keeping templates and plug-ins up to date is too daunting, an even lower-touch solution is **Squarespace**, which makes it truly easy to set up a stunning website specifically designed to support your business -- whether that's a consultancy, an e-commerce site, or a restaurant.

We use Sumo to capture our newsletter signups and the **Newsletter plug-in** to create and send our weekly newsletter. We particularly like Sumo's robust reporting.

We talked a bit about mindfulness and meditation as a way to stay grounded and focused. **Headspace** and **Calm** are apps that newcomers to meditation may find useful.

We also emphasized the importance of self care, and that staying fit and healthy can help make you a better founder. Carole has found the features of her **Fitbit** hugely helpful in this regard -- the hourly reminders to get up and move, the daily and weekly step counts, and especially the achievement badges!

Acknowledgments

We literally would not be still standing as a company without the generosity and kindness of Chip Conley, Karen Wickre, Bart Stephens and Kathi Shreeve.

Our advisors made us bigger and smarter from day one. Hats off to our coach Roy Burstin whose calm wisdom kept us steady through every storm. Our longtime leaders Pam Kramer and Clare Martorana, who kept hiring us in our careers even when we did things very much our own way. The brand-savvy Michela Abrams O'Connor. The smarties Firas (who insisted that it was "the community" - he was right) and Margot Bushnaq who welcomed Jeff in as an Entrepreneur in Residence at Boxador where we were hatched. And Alex Moustoufi who will always pick up the phone.

Tanya Klitch encouraged and edited Jeff's writing at Forbes, where much of these ideas were originally committed to a page.

Our partners amplify our work and we are forever grateful. Deb McDonald at Say What Research. Wendi Burkhardt with Silvernest. Betsy Worley and the inspired leaders of Encore.org, the team at The Modern Elder Academy, Susan Donley at Stria News, Lori Bitter at The Business of Aging, Debbie Weill at Gap Year for Grown-ups Podcast, and Donna Kastner at Retirepreneur.

John, Laura, and Alicia Newton for always being there.

Alexandra Dimiziani who guided our brand story. Neo Tran for bringing our brand to life and for the cover design for this book.

StartOut who believed in us and have made a place to learn and grow for entrepreneurs that others may overlook. A special shout out to Chris Davidson, who coached us on selling when we didn't know what we were even selling.

David and Katherine Allen who have stayed with us as we got things done.

Our investors who stepped up while we were still in the womb: Chip, Bart, Michela, Steve, Sandy, Dino, and Debbie.

And finally, our thanks to good-old Mike Monteiro and the inspiring Erika Hall at Mule Design for the laughs, the example to write about what we're doing and to tell the world why it matters.

www.ingramcontent.com/pod-product-compliance
Lightning Source LLC
Chambersburg PA
CBHW060849220526
45466CB00003B/1296